Miracles
in the
Mess

Affirming God's Truth Daily

TRIBUTE

Copyright © 2017
Tribute Publishing, LLC
Frisco, Texas

Tribute Publishing, LLC

Miracles in the Mess
First Edition December 2017

All Worldwide Rights Reserved
ISBN: 978-0-9982860-8-2

All Rights Reserved. No part of this book may be reproduced, stored in a retrieval system, or transmitted, in any form, or by any means, electronic, recorded, photocopied, or otherwise, without the prior written permission of the copyright owner, except by a reviewer who may quote brief passages in a review.

Printed in the United States of America.

Dedication

I am dedicating this book to my granny, Barbara Ann. Granny, you were always the spiritual rock for our family for so many years. Looking back on my life, you were such an instrumental part of showing God's love and living out his truth every day. You taught me love. Your bold faith, belief in God's miracles, and willingness to share the Hope we have in Jesus will never be forgotten. I am honored to continue this legacy of Faith, Truth and Love.

Miracles in the Mess

Affirming God's Truth Daily
John 8:23

<u>Introduction</u>
In the midst of your mess, it's time to affirm God's truth! Before we get started, I have a few questions for you:

- Do you believe that God is alive today?
- Do you believe that if you call on His name, he WILL show up?
- Do you believe that through Him, ALL things are possible?
- Are you ready to start experiencing the POWER of Christ in your life?

Like really ready? Because I can promise He is waiting to do a mighty work and you are holding the key to the door He has been knocking at.

Here's the deal, I believe that we ALL live messy lives. We are messy people, in a messy world, in need of a Savior. The beautiful thing is, He gets that and He is full of mercy. So often in the mess we get confused, distracted, and just disconnected from our Father. We forget to look for the meaning in the mess.

Confusion, distraction, and discontent lead to isolation, avoidance, and a life less than the one we deserve; the one God has planned for us.

Messiness can either cause us to push away, or it can provide a way for us to LEAN IN to Jesus and look for meaning in the mess.

I sure hope you grabbed this book because you are ready to LEAN IN and start changing the way you look at yourself, your life, and your future. My prayer is that you start shifting your focus to HIS truth.

Learning how to affirm HIS truth in your life is simply life changing if you allow it to be. What you believe about God, His word, and His love for you, ultimately influences where you are in life and what your future holds. As Terri S. Foy says, "What you think about, you bring about." (Proverbs 23:7) If we are speaking lies and negative things to ourselves, then this is the reality in which we live. This becomes our truth. For many years, instead of speaking God's truth over my life, I was listening to my own false declarations, which lead me down a vicious cycle of defeat.

Until a few years ago, the only affirming words that I spoke to myself were *I am not enough, I am not doing enough, and I probably will not ever feel the way I want to feel about myself,* just to share a few. I had trained my brain to assume and think negatively and unfortunately, although it seemed that I was confident and "successful" on the outside,

I continued to feel empty on the inside. It felt like nothing I did was good enough. The things that were going on inside my head were flowing down into my heart and paving a miserable path for me and my life. You see, Matthew 12:34 says your words are a reflection of your heart. My words and "truth" had become lots of lies that were not going to end unless I was willing to spend time with the Lord every day and retrain my brain.

Now I know that you are a lot like me, and according to the National Science Foundation, we have about 12,000-60,000 words that go through our heads each day. Ninety-eight percent are the same thoughts as the day before (especially those of us who are anxious or haven't learned to change our thoughts) and, get this, 80% of all the thoughts we have are negative. This means that most of us have our own personal bully speaking lies to us at any given time during the day. I know I am not alone here, because I have spoken with many of you personally about this, but so few people actually want to take action and change the way they think. We over complicate things or don't even slow down long enough to stop the craziness.

I thank God every day that I was introduced to a new way of thinking, a simple and refreshing way to find Him and his miracles in my every day, and recognizing that His words are my miracles. Seeing ME for who I really am and who I was created to be is often the exact miracle that I needed that day.

I started saying things like *I am enough, I am smart, I am using my God-given gifts to inspire others, I am living with passion and purpose, I am confident and courageous, I know that all things work together for my good…..*

Remember, GOD'S truth is the REAL truth of who God created you to be. It is a declaration of who you really are and where you are headed. Some of these things are your reality, but you have had a foggy mind, so you haven't been able to see the truth. Some of the things are truly right around the corner from your belief.

Miracles in the Mess is dedicated to YOU, the woman who

- often feels overwhelmed and anxious and so desperately needs something to pull you into HIS light every day.
- is on the pursuit of a sense of purpose, but can't see past the fog of everyday life.
- feels somewhat content in your life, but secretly, you feel like there must be more.
- knows God has a bigger plan for your life, but you are fearful to pursue that calling in your heart, so you need His truth every day to give you hope.

Miracles in the Mess is a simple, quick, and refreshing daily HOPE that I desperately needed a few years ago. I started writing His truths out every morning and then the Lord told me that others NEED this too! So, this book is literally a piece of my

heart written to you with LOVE and humility, knowing these words can change your life, too.
I am so humbled and thankful that you are HERE on this journey with Him daily!
Get ready to Affirm God's Truth, sister!

How to Read Miracles in the Mess

- Open the Bible with this book every day and read it! Sounds simple, but sister, if you don't take the time to read it, you are likely to listen to your own lies instead of His truth.
- Verbally, say out loud the declarations of truth and positive affirmations in the large font. This was something that I had never heard of until I was on this pursuit of a better, more God-filled life a few years ago. Thanks to being introduced to Terri S. Foy (terri.com), these little jewels have basically changed my life and the way I think about my life. Take a second to read each affirmation each day, then say it out loud. Affirm THIS truth in your life each day and start to train your brain to think how God wants us to think. (2 Corinthians 10:5)
  - In John 8:31-32, Jesus says, "If you stick with this, living out what I tell you, you are my disciples for sure. Then you will experience for yourself the truth, and the truth will free you." (The Message Bible)
- Start your day with this book, especially with

reading the affirmations, followed by the scripture (this is exactly what I have been doing and THIS simple thing has changes my life dramatically).
- Use this book in conjunction with your Bible when you are stressed or anxious, worried, afraid, or you simply feel like you are being attacked by Satan and you need a tool.
- Using your Bible or Bible app, read and write the scriptures I am suggesting every day. Use a journal in conjunction with this book and journal your thoughts, concerns, frustrations, gratitude, and prayers daily. This is exactly what I started doing and still do EVERY morning. This time is when the Lord showed me my purpose, my dream, and His plan for me. This is how the Lord encouraged me and helped me leave my job and how my marriage was restored... YES, simple, daily scripture reading and writing is when the Lord spoke to me and guided me.
- On each page, I have given you a suggested prayer. This God-inspired prayer is applicable to the specific affirmation for that day and also a sweet opportunity for you to personally talk to your Heavenly Father every day. Share your heart, start with gratitude, and then simply repeat the prayer listed and ask God to be real in your life each day.

ヲ

I am FREE.

I will hold onto You and what You say about me. Jesus, I know that your words are the truth of who I am and the essence of what I was created to be. I know that since I know this truth, I am free.

Thank you, Jesus, that your Word is true and what you say about me is TRUTH. Because I believe this, I know that I am loved, I am forgiven, I am treasured, I am capable, I am an overcomer, I am courageous, I am who you say I am and I will live in this truth. In Jesus' name. Amen.

John 8:31-32; Ephesians 1:7; Romans 8:37

I have the grace to embrace today and every day.

God's grace is sufficient for me (your name), His power is made perfect in my weakness,
so, I delight in them.

Thank you, Jesus, that you never expect me to be all and do all. It is by your grace on which I stand. I know that every detail of my day has purpose. I will rest in your embrace today.
In Jesus' name, Amen.

2 Corinthians 12:9-10

I am highly courageous.

I, (your name), believe every detail of my life of love for God is working out into something good. I am highly courageous in everything that I do because I know this truth. I know that in and through Him, I will live out His purpose.

Thank you, Jesus, that no matter what I am going through, you are working behind the scenes for your own glory and for my good as I'm conformed to Your Son's image. I know you are making my path straight and I can rest assured in this truth. In Jesus' name, Amen.

Romans 8:28-29; Proverbs 3:6

I will start strong and finish stronger.

I will trust God from the bottom of my heart and not try to figure out anything on my own. I will listen for God's voice in everything I do, and everywhere I go, and I know He will direct my path.

Thank you, Jesus, that regardless of my position on this day, I know that I can do all things through your strength in me. It is my desire to work as though I am working for you, in the simple, mundane things and the scary, uncomfortable things. I will strive for excellence because I know that it all matters to you. In Jesus' name, Amen.

Proverbs 3:5-6; Philippians 4:13; Colossians 3:23-24

I will thrive through the trial.

I will be unshakable and assured, deeply in peace. I will experience trouble in this world, but I will take heart, for I know that God has overcome the world.

Thank you, Jesus, that my trial, my storm, my suffering, matters to you. My trial is part of my precious story. All of the details in my story are an opportunity to let you be God in my life. I know that if I lean into you through this storm, you will be my rock and I will thrive.
In Jesus' name, Amen.

John 16:33; James 1:2-3; Psalm 18:2

I am made on purpose for a purpose.

I know that God's rule will prevail.
I will take heart and gain strength.

Thank you, Jesus, that there are specific things that you gave me to do on this earth and these are the very things that you have created me to do. Although I may not see all of these things clearly yet, thank you God for orchestrating every detail of my life and so divinely making things fall into place. Thank you for showing me the way to my purpose. In Jesus' name, Amen.

Habakkuk 3:19; Psalm 27:14;
Proverbs 16:3, 9

I am accepted.

I know that absolutely nothing can separate me from God's love.

Thank you, Jesus, that no matter what I have done, no matter what I will do, you love me anyway. I am fully accepted, and there is nothing that I can do to earn your love. I receive your love today. In Jesus' name, Amen.

Romans 8:39; Ephesians 2:8-9; Romans 15:7

My mind is set to prosper.

The Lord knows what he is doing. He has it all figured out. His plan is to take care of me, not abandon me, to prosper me and give me the future that I hope for.

Thank you, Jesus, that you desire abundance for me. Thank you that you give me the desires I should have. I know that you are taking care of every detail of my life. I know that your plans are greater than my plans. In Jesus' name, Amen.

Jeremiah 29:11; Psalm 37:4; Isaiah 55:8

My mess will be a miracle.

I know that it is a gift when tests and challenges come. I know that when under pressure, my faith-life is forced into the open and shows its true colors. I know it is not wise to try and get out of anything prematurely because through the challenges, I become mature and well developed, not deficient in any way.

Thank you, Jesus, that even through the trial and the struggles, you are able to show yourself and your power. I know that I am not alone in this messy life. Even in the mundane and everyday mess, there are miracles all around. Today, I will look for them. I will see your miracles in my mess. In Jesus' name, Amen.

James 1:2-4; 1 Peter 1:6-7;
Romans 5:3-5; 2 Corinthians 12:9-10

*God is with me,
I cannot fail.*

I know that it was better for Jesus
to die and leave so that His Holy
Spirit is now living in me.

Thank you, Jesus, that when life seems
overwhelming, and I feel like I cannot keep up, I
know that I can keep going. Thank you for showing
me that life isn't about self-striving. Life is about
knowing that because I am living with Christ, I
cannot fail. I might fall, but I cannot fail.
In Jesus' name, Amen.

John 16:7; 2 Corinthians 4:7-10

I know that all things are working together for my good.

I know that God can do exceedingly, abundantly more than I could ever request or imagine.

Thank you, Jesus, that in the midst of the storm, my trials and even everyday life, you have your hand extended to me. I know that you want to be a part of my life and guide me. And even if there is resistance, I know you are working all things for my good. In Jesus' name, Amen.

Ephesians 3:20-21; Romans 8:28-29

I am forgiven.

I know that when I am walking in the light, I experience the Light of God. This light is the cleansing, spotless lamb that purges all sin.

Thank you, Jesus, for showing me that in Christ, I am spotless, I am blameless, and I am forgiven. I know that there is nothing that I have done or anything I will do that can separate me from your love. In Jesus' name, Amen.

1 John 1:7-9; Romans 8:38-39

I am expecting You to show up, God.

I will stay alert, with my eyes wide open with gratitude.

Thank you, Jesus, for being ever-present even today. Since I know that what you promise is true, I will give thanks to God for the things that have come and the things yet to come because of the faith I have in your unchanging ways. I will stay alert and look for You and ways to glorify You today. In Jesus' name, Amen.

Colossians 4:2; Malachi 3:6;
1 Thessalonians 5:16-18

What I speak about, I bring about in my life.

I know that rash language cuts and maims, but there is healing in the words of the wise.

Thank you, Jesus, that you have shown me that my words have power. When I refer to myself as lazy, fat, lacking in energy, less than, not worthy, or that won't ever do something, these words become my reality. What I say literally becomes who I believe I am and what I believe about my life. If I want to change the way I am living my life or change things in my life, I know that I must change the words that are coming out of my mouth. In Jesus' name, Amen.

Proverbs 12:18; Proverbs 15:1

I am not alone.

I know that when I call on the Lord,
he will answer.
He said he will rescue me in bad
times and then honor me.

Thank you, Jesus, that you are a man of your word and what you promise, you do. When I am feeling alone or abandoned, this is simply not true. I recognize that one of Satan's biggest tactics is to make me feel alone and without hope. Today, I choose to hear the truth. Thank you, Jesus, that I am never alone.
In Jesus' name, Amen.

Psalm 91:15; 2 Timothy 4:17;
Jeremiah 29:13

His grace is sufficient.

I know that God's grace is enough; it's all I need. I know that His strength comes into its power through my weaknesses.

Thank you, Jesus, that you have created me. I know that even the things that I consider weaknesses are exactly how you needed me to be. It is through these weaknesses that you can work and shine through me. Help me to embrace my shortcomings and instead surrender my life in your care. In Jesus' name, Amen.

2 Corinthians 12:9-10

His joy comes each morning.

I know that you pile blessings upon me and when I smile, you are glad.

Thank you, Jesus, that your joy is unending, and that there's nothing that can take away my joy, however often I allow things to cover it up. Please continue to help me see you and your blessings, because only through you will joy be complete.
In Jesus' name, Amen.

Psalm 21:6; Psalm 30:5; Psalm 16:11

I am highly favored by God.

I know that whatever I ask for in prayer, I believe that I have received it, and it will be mine.

Thank you, Jesus, that your word is true. That so often I spend so much time trying to figure out how things will work out and simply forget to just ask. I know that you place high value in me and you are listening to me and want the very best for me. For when I ask according to Your will, You are faithful. In Jesus' name, Amen.

1 John 5:14-15; Mark 11:24; James 1:5-8

I am serving others in a unique way.

I know that everything I need to know about pleasing God is found by getting to know Him.

Thank you, Jesus, for hand picking me to love and serve the people that only I can love and serve. Thank you for reminding me that when I get sidetracked or confused about my calling, that the more time I spend with you, the more clear it will become. In Jesus' name, Amen.

2 Peter 1:3; Philippians 2:3; Proverbs 16:9

I am in need of a savior.

I know that if I listen for God's voice in everything I do, everywhere I go, he is the one who will keep me on track.

Thank you, Jesus, for being so real in my life and for showing me the amazing and unique qualities you have given me to use as well as my shortcomings. Thank you for showing me redemption through my need for you. The more I see my need for you, the more real you become.
In Jesus' name, Amen.

Proverbs 3:6; Ephesians 2:1-10

I will stress less, so I am at my best.

I know that I can be content with who I am and know that God's hand is on me, ready to promote me when the time is right. I know that I must stay sober at all times because the devil is waiting to devour me when I get lazy.

Thank you, Jesus, that your hand is on me at all times. Even through the stress, you are here. I know that when things feel out of control, I tend to turn inward and try to fix things. Lord, help me to turn to you so that you can help me glorify You the best way I can. In Jesus' name, Amen.

1 Peter 5:6-10; Matthew 5:25-34

I am confident.

I know that just as the Lord told Aaron to tell the people of His blessings, he also speaks the same for me. I know that he desires to bless me and keep me, for His face to shine on me and to gift me, and to look full in my face and make me prosper.

Thank you, Jesus, for your promises. I know that in YOU I can have abundant life. Because I know your promises, I can have complete confidence in you and my life. You are the source of my confidence. In Jesus' name, Amen.

Numbers 6:22-26

I am a new creation.

I know that when I live God's way, as a new creation, he brings gifts into my life, much the same way as fruits appear in an orchard. Fruits like affection towards others, exuberance for life, and serenity. I develop a willingness to stick to things, a sense of compassion in my heart, and conviction. I find myself in loyal commitments, not needing to force my way into things and I am able to direct my energy wisely.

Thank you, Jesus, that in you, I am a new creation. I know that when I am walking with you, learning more about you, abiding in you, I am different. I am set apart. This vibrant life is my life. In Jesus' name, Amen.

2 Corinthians 5:17; Galatians 5:22-25; Romans 12:2

I laugh without fear of the future.

I wear durable and elegant clothes, and I always face tomorrow with a smile. I am clothed in strength and dignity, and I laugh at the days to come without fear.

Thank you, Jesus, that I do not need to be perfect and that I can laugh without fear of my future. Thank you for pruning me for excellence including my outward appearance so that I can live each day with pride and joy and end each day with a smile. In Jesus' name, Amen.

Proverbs 31:25; John 15:1-4

My foundation is secure.

I belong to God and come from God. I know that I have already won the victory because the spirit of Christ in me is stronger than anything in this world.

Thank you, Jesus, that YOU have overcome the world. I know that my foundation is You. And you are the unwavering, unchanging, eternal God. I know that even though some days it seems so hard, my battles have already been won.
In Jesus' name, Amen.

1 John 4:4; John 16:33

I am strong and courageous.

The Lord says be strong, be courageous. I know that since God is striding ahead of me in anything I do, I need not worry about anything. I know he will not let me down.

Thank you, Jesus, that in you I am strong and capable to fight any battle both spiritual and earthly. I know that you have already given the courage to stand tall and trust. Even though the enemy is out to destroy, I know that you will never leave me or forsake me.
In Jesus' name, Amen.

Deuteronomy 31:6; Joshua 1:6-9

I will not be shaken.

Since everything comes from the Lord,
I will wait as long as I need to
and find rest in you alone.
I know that he is the solid rock and
my salvation, breathing room for my
soul and I will not be shaken.

Thank you, Jesus, for the unshakable ground that I stand upon. Thank you for holding my hand and never letting go. When anxious thoughts start to come, I know that because you are carrying me, I will not be shaken. In Jesus' name, Amen.

Psalm 62:5-6; Matthew 11:28-30;
2 Samuel 22:3

I am fully equipped.

Let the morning bring me your word of your unfailing love; I will go to sleep trusting you. I know that you are pointing me in the right direction, so I am all ears.

Thank you, Jesus, for showing me that when I commit my mornings, my ways to you, you are faithful in directing my path. Thank you for counting me equipped to do all that you have called me to do. I look forward to my mornings with you and the connection that this brings. In Jesus' name, Amen.

Psalm 143:8; Ephesians 2:10

I am safe and secure.

I know that absolutely nothing, nothing living, nothing dead, angelic or demonic, today or tomorrow, high or low, thinkable or unthinkable – NOTHING can get between me and God's love because of the way God has embraced us.

Thank you, Jesus, for saving me. Thank you for redeeming me from all my sins and covering me with your righteousness. I know that no matter what, your embrace is unconditional and everlasting. I know that I am safe and secure, no matter what. In Jesus' name, Amen.

Romans 8:38-39

I am disciplined.

No discipline is fun
and it's often painful.
However, later, I know that it
produces a harvest of righteousness
and peace in myself as I'm being
trained to find myself mature.

Thank you, Jesus, for giving me a disciplined spirit and for showing me that how I do anything is how I do everything. Through the mundane things and the big tasks at hand, I know that what I do each day really matters. Help me to look to you for strength to become more disciplined.
In Jesus' name, Amen.

Hebrews 12:11; 1 Corinthians 10:31

I am made righteous.

I will sing for joy in God, exploding in praise from deep in my soul. For God has dressed me in salvation and given me a robe of righteousness.

Thank you, Jesus, for covering all my sins and considering me righteous. Thank you for placing righteous behind my name, as part of who I am in your eyes. When you look at me, you see excellence, and I will live with a humble joy.
In Jesus' name, Amen.

Isaiah 61:10; Romans 5:1;
2 Corinthians 5:21

His mercies are new every morning.

I know that the Lord hears my cries for mercy and he answers my prayers.

Thank you, Jesus, for having mercy on me. I know that every morning, your mercies are new if I am willing to look to you and receive them. Help me to start my day in expectation of you.
In Jesus' name, Amen.

Lamentations 3:22-23; Psalm 6:9

Today, I will be still.

Be still and know that I am God.

Thank you, Jesus, that you are God and I am not. And thank God I don't have to be. Even though my natural tendency is to do more and strive for more, I know that you are calling me to be still and strive no more. I know that I cannot earn your favor, so I will choose to be still and let you be God. In Jesus' name, Amen.

Psalm 46:10

Today I choose to trust.

I will trust God from the bottom of my heart and not try to figure out anything on my own. I will listen for God's voice in everything I do and everywhere I go, and I know he will direct my path.

Thank you, Jesus, for showing me your truth and your love for me. Thank you for guiding me to the path of daily surrender and trust. For it is in this trust that I am set free. In Jesus' name, Amen.

Proverbs 3:5-6; Psalm 9:10; John 8:36

I am fearless.

I know that there is no fear in love
and well-formed love casts out fear.
And since fear is crippling,
living a fearful life is not one
formed in love.

Thank you, Jesus, for dying for me so that I could experience your fearless love, a love that surpasses all understanding. Thank you for showing me that my fear of death, fear of man, and all other fears are NOT of you. My only fear is a life separated from You. In Jesus' name, Amen.

1 John 4:18; Matthew 10:28;
Proverbs 9:10

I will trust in the trial.

Whatever circumstances I have, wherever I am in my life, I can make it through anything in the one who makes me who I am.

Thank you, Jesus, for you are my ROCK. I know that I can fully trust in you in everything and through everything. No matter what trial I am facing, I choose to trust that you are working behind the scenes for my good and your Glory. In Jesus' name, Amen.

Philippians 4:13

I live life to the fullest.

I am keeping my eyes open for God, watching and waiting for His works. I am alert for his presence.

Thank you, Jesus, for showing up every day in my life. I know that your promises are true and when I seek you, I will find you in all things. I choose to live life KNOWING you are here. I know that there is nothing too small or too big for you.
In Jesus' name, Amen.

Psalm 105:4; Psalm 27:14

I will never be forgotten.

Just as a mother will
never forget her children,
I will never forget you.

Thank you, Jesus, for embracing me, loving me and treasuring me even more than my own mother. I know that I will never be forgotten by you and how amazing and humbling it is to be unconditionally loved this much.
In Jesus' name, Amen.

Isaiah 49:15-16; Psalm 139:13-14

I am treasured.

I know that God has summoned me by name and I am His.

Thank you, Jesus, for choosing me and calling me by name to be your daughter! Despite how I feel, I know I am treasured! I am delicate, unique and precious. In Jesus' name, Amen.

Isaiah 43:1; Proverbs 3:15; Proverbs 31:10

My hope is secure.

I find rest in God alone because my hope comes only from Him.

Thank you, Jesus, that you are here for me always. The hope I am often desperate for is right here with me. And because of my hope in you, I can truly rest. In Jesus' name, Amen.

Psalm 62:5; Psalm 39:7; Psalm 23:1-3

I have the unwavering strength of God.

Yes, indeed – God is my salvation. I trust, I won't be afraid. God – yes God! – is my strength and song, best of all, my salvation!

Thank you, Jesus, that I do not have to rely on my own strength to get through this day, this trial. It is through you that I find refuge and strength beyond my capabilities. I trust you!
In Jesus' name, Amen.

Isaiah 12:2; Exodus 15:2;
Psalm 118:14

I have a calm spirit.

Don't fret or worry. Instead of worrying, pray. Let petitions and praises shape your worries into prayers, letting God know your concerns.

Thank you, Jesus, for showing me that I don't have to be anxious, it's a choice. Fear and anxiety are the opposite of trust, and when I choose this, I am choosing not to trust. I desire a calm spirit, and I know this comes from praying and knowing you. In Jesus' name, Amen.

Philippians 4:6; 1 Peter 5:7; 1 Peter 3:3-4

My light shines for all to see.

I know that God's light will
breakthrough and shine
showing us the way.

Thank you, Jesus, for shining your light on me and
showing me the way. When I feel like I am in the
dark or alone, help me to see it's only Satan's
shadow and you are here. Help me stay in your
light so that I can let my light shine to others.
In Jesus' name, Amen.

Luke 1:78-79; Matthew 5:14-16;
Psalm 119:105

I live a life of freedom.

I know that there is now no condemnation for me because through Christ, the law of the spirit has set me free.

Thank you, Jesus, for setting me free, for dying on the cross and saving me from all unrighteousness. Because of you Jesus, I know that I can live free of guilt, shame or doubt. In Jesus' name, Amen.

Romans 8:1-2

I know all things are possible.

Everything is possible for me if
I truly believe.

Thank you, Jesus, for showing me that through you, all things are possible! Thank you for putting God-sized dreams in my heart that only you can fulfill! I'm looking forward to your blessings!
In Jesus' name, Amen.

Mark 9:23

I am unconditionally loved.

The Lord says I have loved you with an everlasting and unconditional love. No matter what, I'll love you and keep loving you.

Thank you, Jesus, for your love! I know that there are no terms on your part for loving me! You have no expectations of me, and this love is everlasting! Thank you for this gift.
In Jesus' name, Amen.

Jeremiah 31:3

I am victorious.

I give thanks to God because he gives me victory in our Lord Jesus Christ.

Thank you, Jesus, that no matter what I am facing, no matter what is coming, I have victory in your name! You alone are my shield, and I am grateful! In Jesus' name, Amen.

1 Corinthians 15:17;
1 Corinthians 10:13

I am creative.

God does both the making and saving.
He creates each of us by Christ Jesus
to join him in the work he does,
the good work he has gotten ready for
us to do, the work we had
better be doing.

Thank you, Jesus, for giving such wonderful and
unique gifts. The gifts are the way that you desire for
me to serve the world and share you and your love.
In Jesus' name, Amen.

Ephesians 2:10

I am open to change.

"I know what I'm doing. I have it all planned out - plans to take care of you, not abandon you, plans to give you the future you hope for."

Thank you, Jesus, for that even though sometimes my plans are not your plans, I know that ultimately you are directing my path and your plan is for me to prosper. Please help me surrender to your plan.
In Jesus' name, Amen.

Jeremiah 29:11; Isaiah 55:8-9

I am an action taker.

"Yes. I'll stay with you, I'll protect you wherever you go, and I'll bring you back to this very ground. I'll stick with you until I've done everything I promised you."

Thank you, Jesus, for promising that you'll stay with me no matter what. Because of this promise I know that I can take bold actions out of my faith in you. Help me, Jesus, to be bold for your glory. In Jesus' name, Amen.

Genesis 28:15

I am complete.

Dear children, you come from God and belong to God. You have already won a big victory over those false teachers, for the Spirit in you is far stronger than anything in the world.

Thank you, Jesus, that I belong to you! Because of this truth, I know that I truly am complete and lack nothing! I have an abundant life in you and have won the victory over any stronghold on my life! In Jesus' name, Amen.

1 John 4:4; James 1:4; Jeremiah 23:16

I am walking in the way of the Lord.

I will counsel you and teach you in the way you should go; I will counsel you and watch over you.

Thank you, Jesus, for showing me the way. I know that when I am in constant communication with you, I will see, hear and feel the right direction. The more time I spend with you, the more clear the direction. I know that I do not have to worry because I know that I am confidently walking in your ways. In Jesus' name, Amen.

Psalm 32:8

I am overwhelmed with God's goodness.

God Bless You and Keep You, God smile on you and gift you. God look you full in the face and make you prosper.

Thank you, Jesus, for overwhelming me with your goodness. Not a trickle, not a stream, but a flood of blessings. Help me to see all of your goodness in every day. Even through the mess, you are good. In Jesus' name, Amen.

Numbers 6:24-26

I experience the fullness of God.

When you come looking for me,
you'll find me.

Thank you, Jesus, that through you I can experience the fullness of God. When I am intentional about finding you and experiencing your goodness, I know I can.
In Jesus' name, Amen.

Jeremiah 29:13; Psalm 16:11

I am willing to change.

I know that when I get serious about finding and wanting change more than anything, when I come looking, I will find you Jesus.

Thank you, Jesus, for showing me the truth. Sometimes I am just lazy and don't want to change. It's not that you aren't there, it's that I am not looking for you. I know that I must be willing, and where there is a will, I know that You are the way. Help me to be willing.
In Jesus' name, Amen.

Jeremiah 29:13; Psalm 51:12

I am brave.

I will go ahead and be what I was meant to be, I will be brave. Not envious or prideful, and not trying to be something I am not, but BRAVE, ready to fight the good fight with courageous faith.

Thank you, Jesus, for making me brave, for calling me out into the waves so that through you, I become brave. I know that you never promised an easy life, a life without hardship or challenge. Matter of fact, I know that everything that comes into my life has purpose, and through you, I become who you need me to be. I am brave. In Jesus' name, Amen.

Psalm 31:24; Hebrews 13:6

I am unselfish.

Do nothing from selfish ambition or conceit, but in humility count others as more significant than yourselves.

Thank you, Jesus, that you selflessly died for me so that I can have eternal life. Because of your death, I can live under your freedom every day. My tendency is to go about life in a selfish way, especially trying to do everything and figure everything out on my own. Please help me recognize these behaviors and please help me see more of you and less of me.
In Jesus' name, Amen.

Philippians 2:3; Galatians 2:20; Romans 7:15

I have the wisdom of God.

I know that every part of scripture is God-breathed and useful, showing us truth exposing our rebellion, correcting our mistakes, and training us to live God's way.

Thank you, Lord, that you give me all I need in your Word. Thank you that you show me the truth about who I am, you humble me, and show me things I should do differently, and you are truly lovingly training me up in your way through your word. Help me to continue to seek you and cling on to your truth. In Jesus' name, Amen.

2 Timothy 3:16-17

I live without comparison.

Am I trying to win the approval of human beings or God? Am I trying to please people? If I am trying to please people, I am not a servant of God.

Thank you, Jesus, for setting the example of an authentic life. You lived the right way regardless of what others thought and you loved no matter what. Help me to listen to only You and your opinion of me. Help me to not get distracted by flashy things or opinions. I am here to shine your light and to please you only.
In Jesus' name, Amen.

Galatians 1:10

I am loved.

For God loved me so much that he gave his one and only son, so that whoever believed in him should not perish, but have eternal life.

Thank you, Jesus, for sending your son to die an innocent death for me. I know that you love me so much and because of your death, I am free. Thank you for your forgiveness, and saving me. I know that you love me no matter what. No matter what I have done, or I am going to do, your love covers it all. I am loved. In Jesus' name, Amen.

John 3:16

I am obedient.

Good work! You did your job well. You have been faithful in handling the small things, so now I will give you more responsibility.
From now on, be my partner.

Thank you, Jesus, for showing me that my obedience, no matter in small things or big things, always pays off. Thank you for acknowledging my works, for being proud of me, and also for reminding me that everything counts. I will continue to follow you, to strive for excellence, and know that you are my biggest fan. In Jesus' name, Amen.

Matthew 25:21; 1 Corinthians 10:31

I attract God-inspired ideas.

I am filled with your Spirit, so I know that you have given me your wisdom and the abilities and expertise in the specific areas I am gifted in. I acknowledge that my gifts are from you and that you give me ways to use these ideas to bring you glory and create abundance in my life.

Thank you, Jesus, for gifting me with a desire to be the light. I know that you have given me unique gifts and ideas that you have placed on my heart. I know that these things come from you! Help me to be bold and lean into these God-inspired ideas, for they have a sparkle of light that you want to use to reach others for your glory. Continue to flood my mind and heart with your God-sized dreams and ideas. In Jesus' name, Amen.

Romans 12:6-8

I am comfortable being uncomfortable.

I will trust in your unfailing love;
my heart rejoices in your salvation.

Thank you, Jesus, for constantly putting me into situations that create uncomfortableness. I know that you love me so much and that you desire my complete dependence. Help me to recognize comfort, as well as the things in life that allow me to get uncomfortable, as gifts and blessings allowing me to grow closer to you and into the person you have created me to be. I trust you, Jesus, and your love for me.
In Jesus' name, Amen.

Psalm 13:5; Romans 5:3-5; James 1:2-4

I am beautiful.

Charm is deceptive, and beauty is fleeting; but a woman who fears the Lord is to be praised.

Thank you, Jesus, for captivating my heart and soul, for helping me realize that my outward beauty is truly fleeting. As much as I want to be well kept, I know that your only concern is my heart and my pursuit of you. I also know that you have made me perfect and you consider me a prized possession. Please help me to remember how valued I am and help me to live as the beautiful soul that I am. In Jesus' name, Amen.

Proverbs 31:30; 1 Peter 3:3-4; 1 Corinthians 6:19-20

I dream BIG dreams.

I sought the Lord and he delivered me from ALL my fears.

Thank you, Jesus, for putting dreams in my heart. Thank you for breaking down walls of fear and doubt and making your plans clear to me. Thank you for revealing yourself to me through your Word and for showing that anything is possible through You. Thank you for giving me ambition to go for the things you want me to do and for showing up time and time again. I dream big dreams. In Jesus' name, Amen.

Psalm 34:4

I am focused.

If I put on the full armor of God,
I can stand firm against
the schemes of Satan.

Thank you, Jesus, for transforming my mind and allowing me to focus. With so many distractions around us every day, every moment, I know that I can stay focused. When I put on the armor of God each day, I know that I can stand firm. I know that I can have self-control and patience. I know I can stay focused on the task at hand. As often as I become distracted, I know that I am focused. I put my head down and I can get the job done.
In Jesus' name, Amen.

Ephesians 6:10-18; Romans 12:2;
1 Thessalonians 5:8

I live a good life.

I know that if I just keep going and do not grow weary, I will reap a reward if I do not give up.

Thank you, Jesus, for running this race of life with me. You have placed so many things and people in my life that remind me just how good life is when we are living a faith-filled life. When we truly know that all things are working for our good, we have no need to get stressed. Help me to live more freely by spreading Your Word, doing good, and trusting in you. In Jesus' name, Amen.

Galatians 6:9; Hebrews 12:1-3

I am a beautiful masterpiece.

I know that my body is a temple of the Holy Spirit, and he is living in me. I know that I am not my own.

Thank you, Jesus, that no matter the state of health I am in, you desire me to be full of joy and thankful. You want me to recognize that my body is a vessel that you want to use for your glory.
Even when I don't feel well or feel capable, provide me with your strength, your energy, and your perspective. You know where I am, God. My situation matters to you and I trust you will use my situation and story. I know that my body is a temple and your desire for me is be ready and prepared to be used however you see fit. Please help me be ready and prepared to be used.
In Jesus' name, Amen.

1 Corinthians 6:19; 2 Timothy 4:2; Peter 3:15

I am filled with the peace of God.

I know that He restores my soul, my mind, my will, and my emotions.

Thank you, Jesus, that you are ever present. Even in the midst of the busy schedules, demanding kids and jobs, you are present. I know that when I choose to sit with you, listen, be grateful, and wait on you, you restore my soul. My mind, my will, and my emotions can be restored and rejuvenated in you. In Jesus' name, Amen.

Psalm 23:1-3

I will rise early to give God control of my day.

Lord, you hear my voice, at daybreak, I plead my cause to you and I wait in expectation.

Thank you, Jesus, for calling me to your side early in the morning. Even though some mornings it seems impossible to get up, I know that you are waiting and you will help me. Each day that I give you control and await in expectation for you, these days are my best days. Help me to remember that when I rise and give you my days, this is an act of discipline that is rewarded and loved by you. In Jesus' name, Amen.

Psalm 5:3

I can avoid all distraction.

I know that if I cry out,
God hears me.

Thank you, Jesus, that you have given me a spirit of discipline to take action and avoid all distraction. Distractions are coming from all sides in comparison, shiny objects, impatience, weariness, the list can go on as to what distracts us, God. But you know them all. Distraction and isolation is one of Satan's tactics to keep me from having peace and I know that all too well. Help me to see things as they are and give me the capacity to stay focused. I know you will help me stay focused. In Jesus' name, Amen.

Psalm 34:17-18; 2 Timothy 1:7

I am impacting the world for Jesus in a unique way.

I know that through spending time with you Jesus, I am filled with hope, joy, and peace. Through these things, you are creating a radiant life-giving energy in me through the Holy Spirit so that this light in me brings YOUR hope to others. This Hope allows me to impact the world for you.

Thank you, Jesus, for your Word, for speaking directly to me, for loving me, and constantly holding my right hand. I know that you have specific things you have called me to do here on earth. I recognize these things are unique to me and you are fully equipping me to do them. Through you, Jesus, I know that I am impacting the world in YOUR way. Thank you for this gift and for your guidance as I am allowed amazing opportunities to serve you. In Jesus' name, Amen.

Romans 15:13

I am a voice of encouragement.

I believe that it is my duty as the daughter of the Most High King to display a loving and kind character at all time. I also realize that this is near impossible without the Holy Spirit. Through Him, I will speak words of encouragement. I will build up and show love to those around me.

Thank you, Jesus, for giving me life and for giving us your Word of truth. I fall short, I grow weary, but you never do. You call me into your arms to refresh and satisfy me. Because of your grace and mercy, I am learning to love you and love myself. When I understand your love, Jesus, I know that it is my duty to encourage others and to share your light and love.
This is what we are here to do.
I am a voice of encouragement.
In Jesus' name, Amen.

1 Thessalonians 5:11, 14

I stay focused on my priorities.

If I cast my cares on the Lord, he will sustain me. No matter what you have called me to do, you are my strength. My priority is honoring You and bringing glory to your name through loving others and being obedient.

Thank you, Jesus, for giving me such a beautiful life. It is easy to get distracted with all the things that I believe you have called me to do and often I feel overwhelmed. Naturally, I start focusing on why I can't do certain things instead of focusing on your promise to sustain me, to walk with me, and guide me, to hold me up and be my refuge and strength. For I know there is nothing that I cannot do if you are in it. Help me to seek you and honor the tasks of service that you have given to me, in my home and in the world.
Jesus, you are my everlasting companion.
In Jesus' name, Amen.

Psalm 55:22

I am friendly.

Anyone who withholds kindness from a
friend, forsakes the fear
of the Almighty.

Thank you, Jesus, for your loving kindness. Thank you for showing me how to love and how to be friendly. There are so many hurting and lonely people who need a friend, someone who needs to know about you and your love. Help me to be kind and willing to be available to those who need a friend. In Jesus' name, Amen.

Job 6:14

I am blessed to be a blessing.

"In everything I did, I showed you that by this kind of hard work we must help the weak, remembering the words the Lord Jesus himself said: 'It is more blessed to give than to receive.'"

Thank you, Jesus, that because of your grace, I am blessed beyond comprehension. Each day is full of your goodness if I am willing to look for it. You teach me that it is better to give out of love and humility, knowing that is what you called us to do. We are more blessed by what we give and do for others than what we have.
In Jesus' name, Amen.

Acts 20:35

My voice proclaims the name of Jesus.

> I will declare your name to my
> people, in the assembly
> I will praise you.

Thank you, Jesus, for giving me a voice. You have saved me and brought me into your light and I will boast and share your glorious name boldly. My voice can impact multitudes and help shape the hearts of the future. Through you Jesus, my voice will proclaim your name. In Jesus' name, Amen.

Psalm 22:22

I avoid evil.

He tests the good and the bad alike,
if anyone cheats, God is outraged.
God's business is making
things right.

Thank you, Jesus, for your grace and mercy. I know that you hate evil, you hate lying, cheating, and stealing to name a few. For I know that I have fallen short and sin against you many times, yet you still love me and call me back into your arms. Help me to recognize evil, to turn from it, and help others do the same by declaring your truth. I avoid all evil. In Jesus' name, Amen.

Psalm 11:5-6; Psalm 13:2-3;
1 Thessalonians 5:22

I am an encourager.

Those who are stronger and able in the faith need to step in and lend a hand to those who falter, and not just do what is most convenient. Strength is for service, not for status.

Thank you, Jesus, that the more time I spend with you, the stronger I become. I have learned that so many people just need you and your love and I don't have to be perfect to encourage someone. Matter of fact, when I unselfishly love and encourage others, my heart is content. You created me to be the light and to share your light. I find joy in being an encourager.
In Jesus' name, Amen.

Romans 15:1-2

I love like Christ loves.

Greater love has no one than this: to lay down one's life for one's friend. You are my friends if you do what I command. I no longer call you servant, instead I call you friend for everything I have learned, I have shared with you.

Thank you, Jesus, for laying down your life for me. You died an undeserving death so that I can live a life of freedom and have life eternal. I know that through you, I have access to your truth, your love, your way. You hold nothing back. Because of this great love for me, my heart's desire is to love like you love: a selfless, unconditional love that surpasses all human understanding. This love is hard, because I am selfish. Please help me to see others like you see them and to love how you love. In Jesus' name, Amen.

John 15:13-15

I use my gifts to help people.

We have different gifts, according to the grace given to each of us. If your gift is prophesy, then prophesy in accordance to your faith, if it is serving, then serve, if it is teaching, then teach, if it is encouraging, then encourage, giving, then give, leading, then diligently lead, mercy, give it cheerfully.

Thank you, Jesus, for your precious and unique gifts that you have given me. You gave them to me to use for your glory and they bring me great joy. When I think about what makes me feel the best in life, it is always when I am using my gifts to glorify You and when I am sharing you with others. Thank you for giving me opportunities daily to use my God-given gifts. Help me to be more aware of when others need me.
In Jesus' name, Amen.

Romans 12:6-9

I am humble.

Oh my soul, bless God, and don't forget a single blessing. I know that living with humility is how you are able to use me. I throw off all spoiled virtue and in simple humility, allow you God, the great gardener, to make a vibrant salvation-garden of my life.

Thank you, Jesus, for every opportunity, for every trial, every good and perfect gift which all comes from you. I am so grateful. Life gets messy and hard, but you know this God. Help me to see the good in every day and recognize your faithfulness and guidance in it all. In Jesus' name, Amen.

James 1:21

I am an eager learner.

Every part of scripture is God-breathed and useful one way or another - showing us truth, exposing our rebellion, correcting our mistakes, training us to live God's way.

Thank you, Jesus, that you make your truth, your way, available to us in the Bible. I know that your plans for me are vast and abundant and you want unimaginable blessings for me in my life. I also know that life is a journey of learning and seeking and often making mistakes. Thank you that your word is my lamp and I know that I can trust you and your ways above anything. I am eagerly willing to learn and seek you, because I know I will find you. In Jesus' name, Amen.

2 Timothy 3:16-17; Psalm 119:105; Jeremiah 29:13

I have the security and peace of God.

I know when I see my life in God-reality, God-initiative, and under God's provision, I don't have to worry about missing out. I know all of my human needs will be met.

Thank you, Jesus, that my security can and should be found in you alone. When I am anxious, overwhelmed, unsure, and doubting, I know that when I see you and your way I will have all of my needs met. Please help me to not look to the things of this world or other people in my life for the peace that I so long for, rather fix my eyes on you. In Jesus' name, Amen.

Matthew 6:33

I have an unquenching thirst for God's truth.

When I don't know what I am doing, I know that all I have to do is pray to Jesus. He loves to help, and I will get the help I need and won't be condescended when I ask.

Thank you, Jesus, for your unconditional love for me. Thank you for being instantly available when I seek you and ask for your help. Thank you for your grace and your mercy every day.
You don't judge me, rather you encourage my communication with you. I know that in the time I spend with you that my questions and concerns will be addressed, and I will have clarity and more peace in my life. Your word is the truth of who I am. I thirst for your truth. In Jesus' name, Amen.

James 1:5; John 4:14

I am anchored in God's truth.

Then Jesus turned to the Jews who claimed to believe him and said, "If you stick with this, living out what I tell you, you are my disciples for sure. Then you will experience and know the truth, and the truth with set you free."

Thank you, Jesus, that you reveal yourself and your love for me through your word. The more I read it and the more time I spend with you, the richer and clearer my understanding is of you. Knowing your truth, what you say about me, and who I am in you, brings true peace and freedom. I will cling to you and your words.
In Jesus' name, Amen.

John 8:31-32

I manifest God's everyday miracles.

God, I know that you are ready and waiting to shine your goodness, your miracles on me. Your greatest gift is saving me. It was your idea and I know that I must trust you enough to let you do what you want to do in my life.

Thank you, Jesus, that you gifted me with many miracles. So often I am so distracted with the tasks of the day that I overlook the miracles you are trying to show me, like experiences with family and our children, and Your provision in our home, food, friends, and clothes. Forgive me for overlooking even the small things, there are things that you have divinely given me to do, and you are working miracles in each of these everyday activities and tasks. Help me to live in a way that you are on display in my everyday life. In Jesus' name, Amen.

Psalm 77:11, Ephesians 2:8-10

I am leaving a magnificent impact on this world.

God, I know that you chose me to impact the world in a unique way. I know that through you, I can find my meaning and function and I can impact the world through you, Jesus.

Thank you, Jesus, that you designed my fingerprints to be like no one else. That you have called me to a magnificent purpose, which means to leave a magnificent impact. You said that my past, my circumstances are designed to be used for my good and your glory. I know that you have orchestrated my life in such a way that I am to use my God-given gifts and talents. I know that I am leaving a magnificent impact.
In Jesus' name, Amen.

Romans 12:6; Matthew 5:14-16; Romans 8:28-29

I am a mighty vessel.

God, I know that you are the true vine, my source of life, and I am a branch that extends from you. Without you, I am nothing. I know that when I am joined with you, being nourished by you, the harvest is plenty.

Thank you, Jesus, that you allow me access to your power, your might, and your presence. I know that my primary role on this earth is to be the light to share you, your love, your grace, and your hope. I know that if I allow you to use me, lives can be changed. In you, Jesus, I am a mighty vessel. In Jesus' name, Amen.

John 15:5-8; Matthew 5:14-16

I am anchored in love.

God, you commanded us to love one another. Not just a simple, surface love, but love others the way that you have loved us. When I love this way, it is bold, noticeable, and recognizable as coming from you.

Thank you, Jesus, that you have shown me how to love. You commanded me to love, above all else. Lord, I confess that often I can place judgement and question if I am loveable and if other people are even worthy of love, I am sorry. I desire to love whole heartedly and strive for unconditional love towards myself and others just as you have given this to me. Help me to look beyond the circumstances and just know that you have put me here on this earth to display an agape love. I affirm that I am anchored in your love, and I will spread it like wildfire. In Jesus' name, Amen.

John 13:34-35

About the Author

Cheneil is a full-time professional motivator, faith-based lifestyle coach, mentor, and speaker. She resides in Texas with her husband of 13 years and two preschool boys.

She is an outgoing, energetic, daughter of the King who loves fitness and Jesus. She is passionate about helping women like you understand God's truth, His unconditional, unwavering love for you, and helping you see it and live in it in the midst of your everyday messy life.

Through her time caring for patients as a Certified Acute Care Nurse Practitioner for over a decade, the Lord started to reveal His truth to her in a defining, real, and raw way, and in the midst of a messy, exhausting, and dry time in her life.

Out of this confusing and desperate time, Miracles in the Mess was born.

Cheneil's heart is for YOU, encouraging you, and motivating you through your mess. Because it's through this mess that God is making Miracles.

She shares her heart and passion with you in many ways:

- Monthly Interactive Faith Calendar: includes a community of women who need a plan, encouragement, and accountability. You can experience daily LIVE devotion videos as well as a daily complementary fitness circuit to start honoring the Lord with your body and get your motivation juices flowing in a private online group.
- Individualized Faith-Based Online Lifestyle Coaching to help you on a more personal level.
- Motivational Faith-Based Speaking on Lifestyle & Healthy Living for your next Women's event.

Motivating you through His Grace & Love,

Cheneil

Learn more at cheneiltorbert.com
or
Follow her on Facebook at The Momma Motivator

Disclaimer & Copyright Information

The author and publisher have made every effort to ensure that the information in this book was correct at press time, the author and publisher do not assume and hereby disclaim any liability to any party for any loss, damage, or disruption caused by errors or omissions, whether such errors or omissions result from negligence, accident, or any other cause.

All quotes, unless otherwise noted,
are attributed to the author.

Cover illustration, book design and production
Copyright © 2017 by Tribute Publishing LLC
www.TributePublishing.com

Scripture references are copyrighted by
www.BibleGateway.com which is operated by the
Zondervan Corporation, L.L.C

www.ingramcontent.com/pod-product-compliance
Lightning Source LLC
Chambersburg PA
CBHW021131300426
44113CB00006B/380